OVER

2001
Ultimate
Stickers
for Boys

igloobooks
.com

Digger Drawing

Use your best pens to make these two pictures of the digger look exactly the same.

Driver Dilemma

Can you match each of the drivers to their vehicles?

b truck

1 delivery driver

2 farmer

3 builder

a digger

c tractor

Matching Mighty Movers

Can you match the pairs of vehicles? Which vehicle does not have a pair?

a b c d e f g h i j k l m n o p q

JOKE CORNER

Q. Why don't traffic lights ever go swimming?

A. Because they take too long to change!

Construction Site Counting!

Can you count how red, blue & yellow vehicles are in this picture? Write your answers in the circles below.

a red

b blue

c yellow

Mixed up Mixers

Look very carefully at the jumbled picture below.
How many cement mixers can you count?

Jumbled Jigsaws

Can you spot which pictures complete this digger jigsaw?

a

b

c

d

e

Spot the Difference

Can you spot the **5** differences between these two pictures?
Circle them as you spot them!

a

b

Maze Master

Can you work out which way the bulldozer should go to collect his load of rubble?

Digger Drawing

Draw a cool digger! Copy the picture square by square into the big grid below, then decorate it with your best pens and pencils.

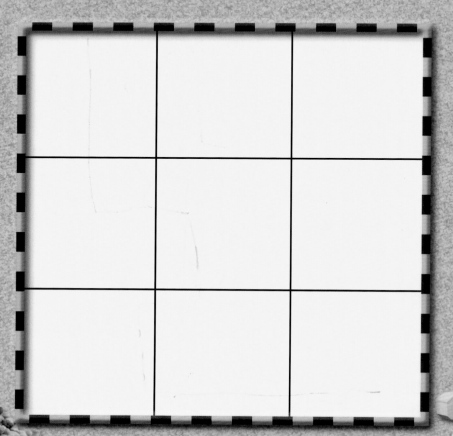

Paper Tractor Picture

1. Ask an adult to cut a strip of green paper. Use the glue to stick this at the bottom of the blue piece of paper.

You will need:
- Scissors
- Green, black, yellow and blue craft paper
- PVA Glue

2. Ask an adult to cut a rectangle and a square from the yellow paper. Glue it on the blue paper, as shown.

3. Ask an adult to cut a square from the blue paper that is smaller than the square of yellow paper. Glue this in place, as shown.

4. Ask an adult to cut two circles from the black paper, one should be smaller than the other. Glue the wheels to the tractor, as shown.

5. Finally, ask an adult to cut two thin rectangles from the black paper. Glue them on for the roof and the exhaust, as shown. You could even use your pens to add in more detail.

Construction Site Photos

The site manager has taken close-up photos around the site.
Can you work out which photo belongs to each vehicle?

Shadow Match

Only one of these shadows matches the picture of the digger.
Can you spot which one it is?

a

b

c

d

e

Whirling Wheels

These wheels have all become jumbled up.
Draw lines between each matching pair and then circle
the one without a pair.

Digger Driver

Which line of the cones will get the builder to his digger the fastest?
The fewer the cones, the faster he will get there.

a

b

c

Brilliant Bulldozers

Follow these easy steps to draw a bulldozer.

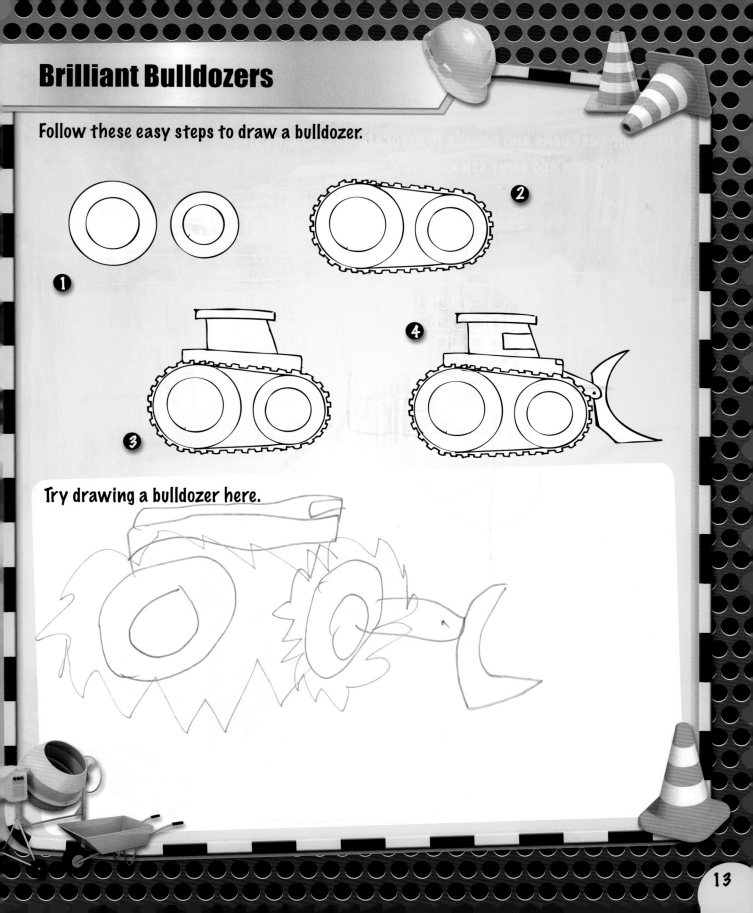

Try drawing a bulldozer here.

Design your own Building Site

Use your best pens and pencils to decorate this building site.
You could even add some stickers, too!

JOKE CORNER
Q.What do you call someone who used to be really keen on tractors?

A. An extractor fan!

14

Master the Maze

Can you help the driver find his way out of the maze to his truck?

Half and Half

Use your best pens and pencils to finish these pictures.

Match the Pair

Can you match each pair of cement mixers? Which is the odd one out?

Vehicle Madness

Look very carefully at these two pictures. Can you spot which vehicle is in picture 1 but not in picture 2? Can you see the extra vehicle in picture 2?

Cardboard Big Rig

You will need:

- A thin cardboard box
- Craft paper
- Bottle tops
- Pens
- Sticky tape
- PVA glue

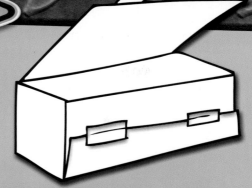

1. Cover the thin card box in craft paper and stick in place using sticky tape, as shown in picture a.

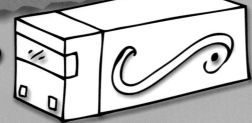

2. Use a felt pen to draw on the cab and a cool design down the side, as shown in picture b.

3. Glue the bottle tops to your cardboard box for the wheels, as shown in picture c.

4. Wait until the glue has dried before playing with your truck. Why don't you try making different types of vehicles.

Tractor Twins

Only two of these tractors match.
Can you spot which ones?

a

c

e

b

d

Shadow Match

Can you spot which shadow matches the bulldozer?

a

b

c

d

e

20

Machine Maths

Each of these groups of tools can be added to at least one other group to make 7 tools in total. Can you spot which groups should be added together?

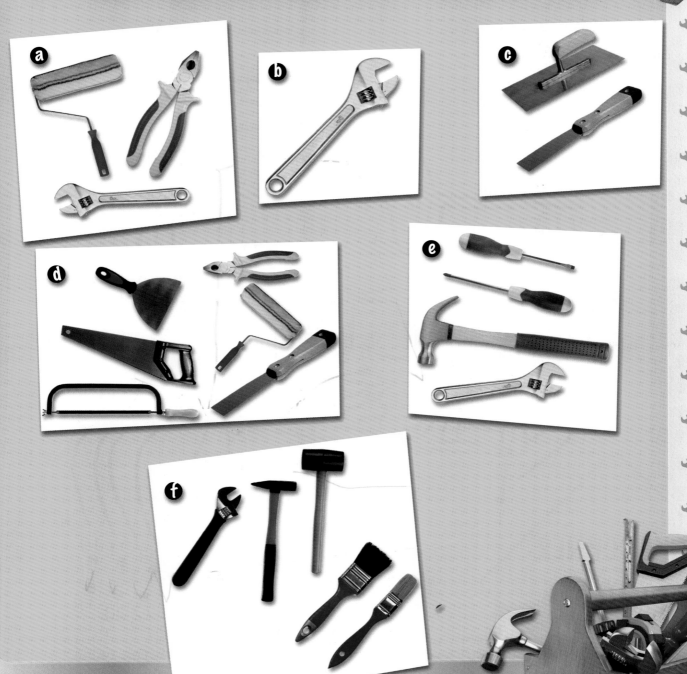

Dot- to-Dot

Join the dots and discover a cool vehicle! Use your best pens and pencils to decorate it.

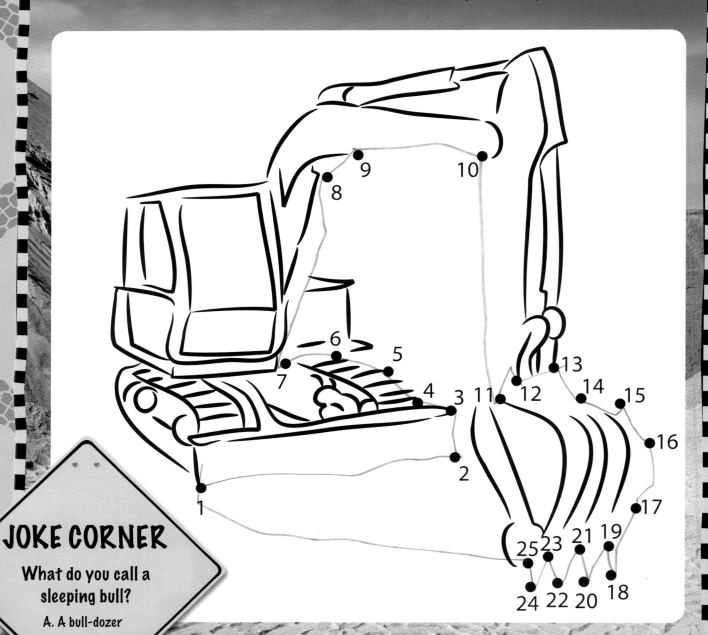

JOKE CORNER

What do you call a
sleeping bull?

A. A bull-dozer

Digger Duos

Can you match the drivers to the diggers by following the lines?

Spot the Difference

Can you spot the **5** differences between these two cool pictures?
Circle them as you find them.

Beastly Bugs

Can you count how many different bugs there are in this creepy crawly picture? Write your answers in the white boxes below.

Worm	Ladybug	Ant	Spider	Fly	Dragonfly	Butterfly

Hiding Places

Follow the lines to discover where each bug likes to hide most.

a.

b.

c.

d.

e.

1.

2.

3.

4.

5.

Mega Moths

Make a cool mega moth paper chain!

You will need:

Pencil
Paper
Scissors
Crayons/Pens

1. Take a long piece of card and fold it backwards and forwards like a concertina, as shown.

2. On the top section, draw a moth whose wings touch each of the edges of the paper, as shown.

3. Ask an adult to carefully cut around your moth.

4. Decorate them using your best pens and crayons.

JOKE CORNER

Q. What's the biggest moth in the world?

A. A mammoth!

Bug Patterns

Can you work out which bug should come next in each of these patterns? Draw them in when you have worked it out.

1.

2.

3.

4.

5.

Beetle Match

Only one of these shadows matches this beetle.
Can you spot which one it is?

a.

b.

c.

d.

e.

Which Way?

Can you work out which trail the ant should follow to find the yummy apple?

a.

b.

c.

Memory Game

Study this picture for 30 seconds. Cover it over and then see if you can answer the questions at the bottom of the page.

1. How many spiders were there?
2. How many wings did the dragonfly have?
3. Did you see a ladybug?
4. How many beetles were there?

JOKE CORNER

Q. What do you get if you cross a centipede and a parrot?

A. A walkie talkie!

Picture Perfect

Use the grids to help you copy these cool creepy crawlies.
Decorate them using pens and pencils.

Bug Body Parts

Follow the dot-to-dots to finish the missing parts of these bugs.
Now use pens to decorate the pictures.

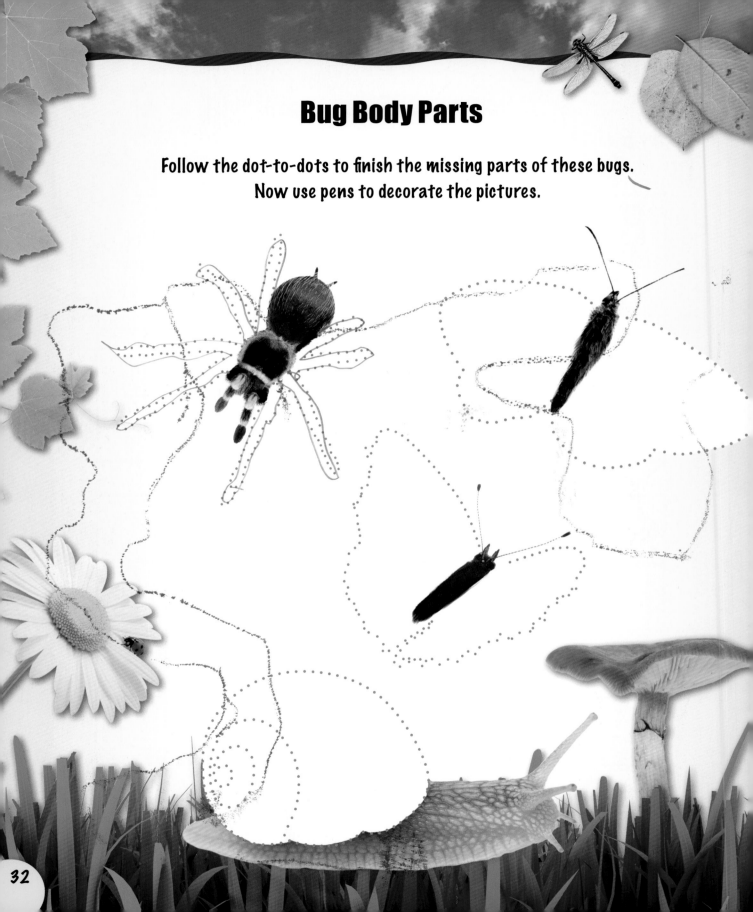

Mega Maze

Can you help the ant find its way to the juicy leaves?

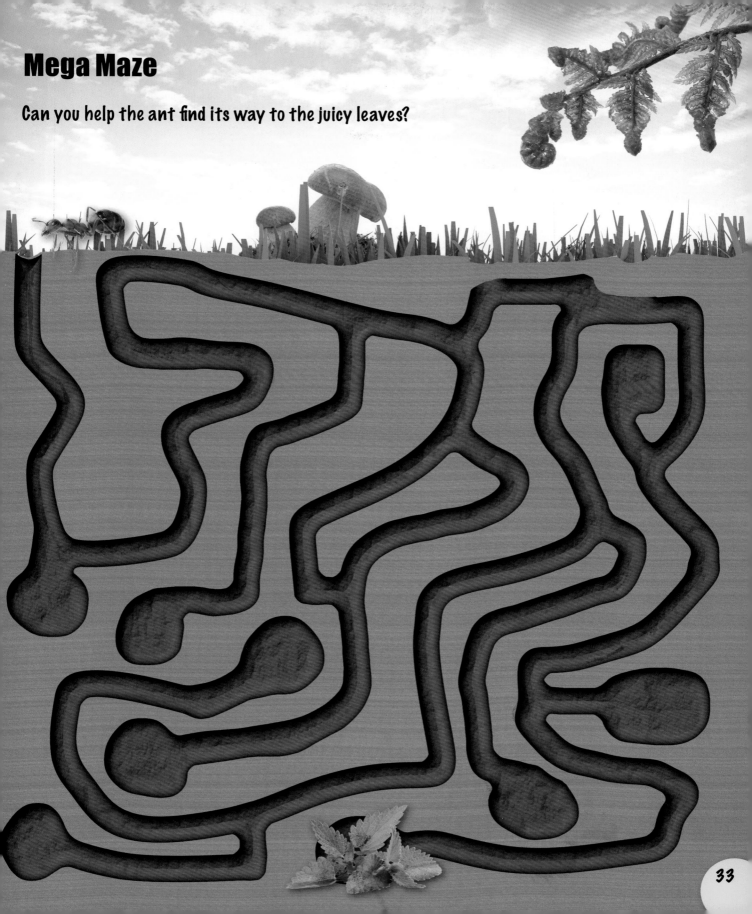

Tarantula Twins

Can you spot which two of these tarantulas are exactly the same?

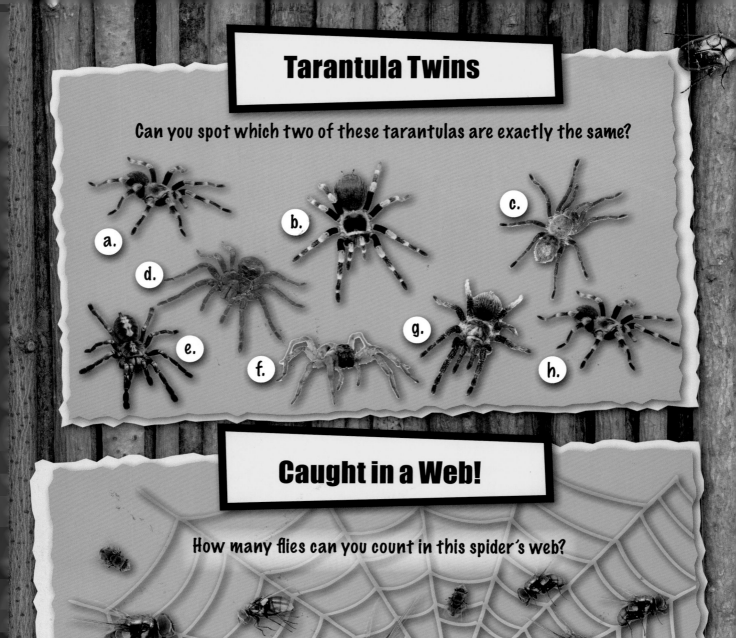

a.

b.

c.

d.

e.

f.

g.

h.

Caught in a Web!

How many flies can you count in this spider's web?

Incredible Insects

Use these sets of legs to draw some imaginary bugs. They could have two heads, or a big spiky stinger! Once you've drawn them, you can use your pens to decorate them.

JOKE CORNER

Q. What do you call a snail without a home?

A. A slug

Paper Plate Beetle

You will need:

- Three paper plates
- Red, black and white paint
- Black card
- Scissors
- PVA Glue

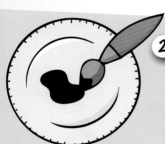

1. Cut the circle out of one of the paper plates and paint it black.

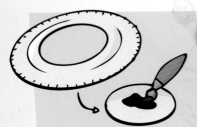

2. Paint the second paper plate black.

3. Cut the third plate in half and paint both pieces red. When dry add some black dots.

4. Glue the red halves to the black paper plate body and then glue the black circle underneath to make the face, as shown.

5. To finish, paint a face on your bug and add 6 construction paper legs.

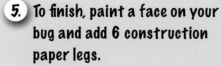

36

Spectacular Stag Beetles

Follow these easy steps to draw a stag beetle.

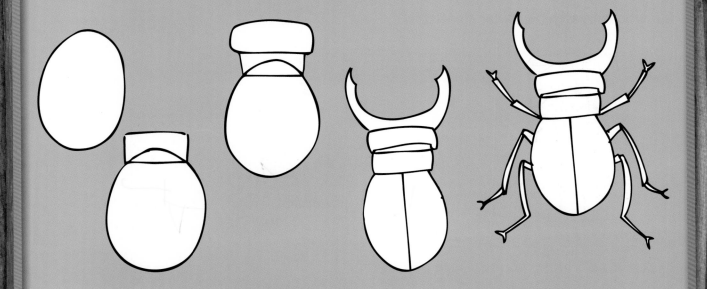

Try drawing some stag beetles here.

Catch the Fly

The spiders are racing to the spider's web,
but who will catch the fly for dinner first?

Players: 2-4

You will need: Coins to use as counters and a die

Instructions:

Each player should choose a spider sticker from
the sticker sheets and stick it to their counter.
Place the counters on the start space.
Take it in turns to roll the die and move
your counter forward that many of spaces.
If you land on an ant, you can move
forward one space.
If you land on a toadstool
you must move back two spaces.
The first spider to land on
the spider's web wins!

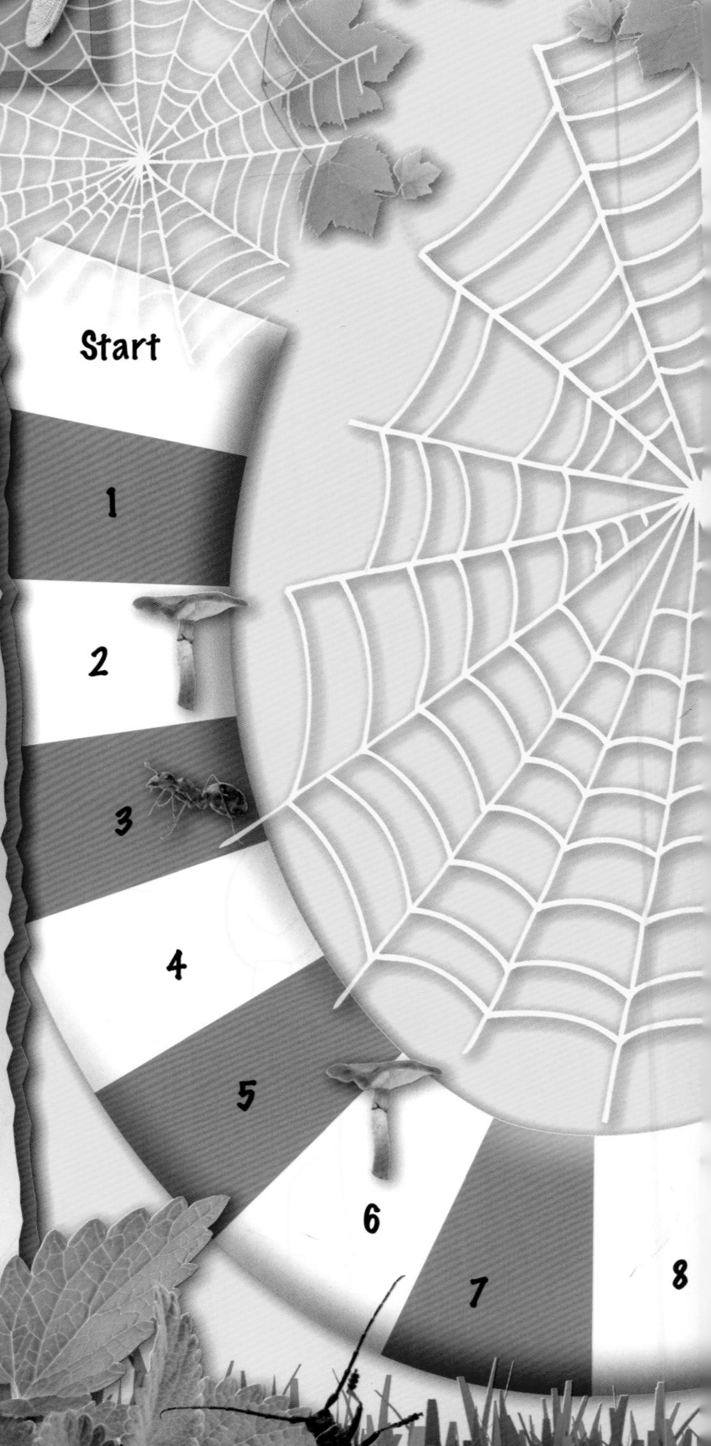

Start

1

2

3

4

5

6

7

8

10 11 12 13 14 15 16 17 18 19 20 21 22 23 24 25 26 27 28 29 30 Finish

Creepy Crawlies

Can you count how many different bugs there are in this creepy crawly picture? Write your answers in the white boxes below.

Scary Spiders!

Follow these easy steps to draw a super cool spider!

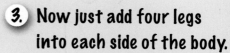

1. Start by drawing a face with fierce jaws.

2. Add the body.

3. Now just add four legs into each side of the body.

Try drawing a spider here.

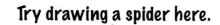

Honeycomb Maze

Can you help this buzzy bee find his way through the
honeycomb maze to his friend at the other side?

Make a Bumblebee

1. Paint the paper plate yellow and let it dry.

2. With black paint or markers, add on stripes.

3. Use a marker to draw a face onto the plate.

4. Cut two wings out of waxed paper and attach these with sticky tape.

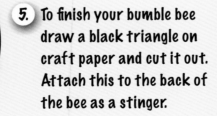

5. To finish your bumble bee draw a black triangle on craft paper and cut it out. Attach this to the back of the bee as a stinger.

Odd Wasp Out

Can you spot which of these wasps is the odd one out?
What is different about it?

a.

b.

c.

d.

e.

f.

g.

h.

Spider Tangle

How many spiders can you count in this jumbled picture?

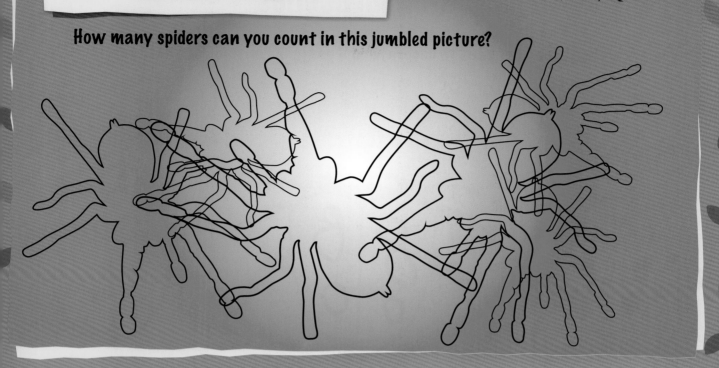

Beastly Bugs

Can you spot the matching pairs of bugs?

a.

b.

c.

d.

e.

f.

g.

h.

i.

j.

k.

l.

m.

n.

45

Brilliant Beetles

Use your best pens to decorate cool patterns on each of these beetles.

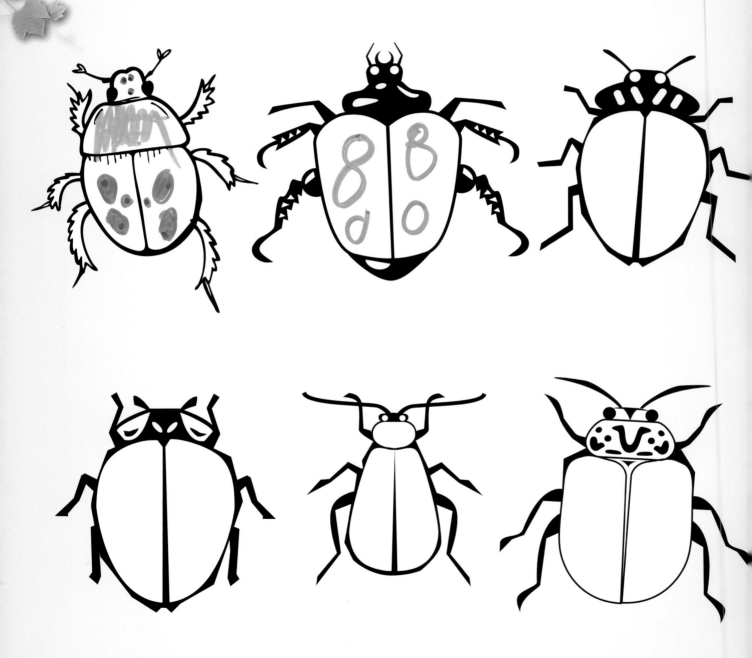

Dino Drawing

Use your pens to complete these deadly dino pictures.

Camarasaurus Clues

One of these dinosaurs is a Camarasaurus. Follow the clues below to work out which one it is. Write your answer in the white box below.

a.

b.

c.

d.

e.

Clue 1. The Camarasaurus cannot fly.

Clue 2. The Camarasaurus walks on four legs.

Clue 3. The Camarasaurus does not have spines on its back.

Clue 4. The Camarasaurus has a long neck.

Letter D

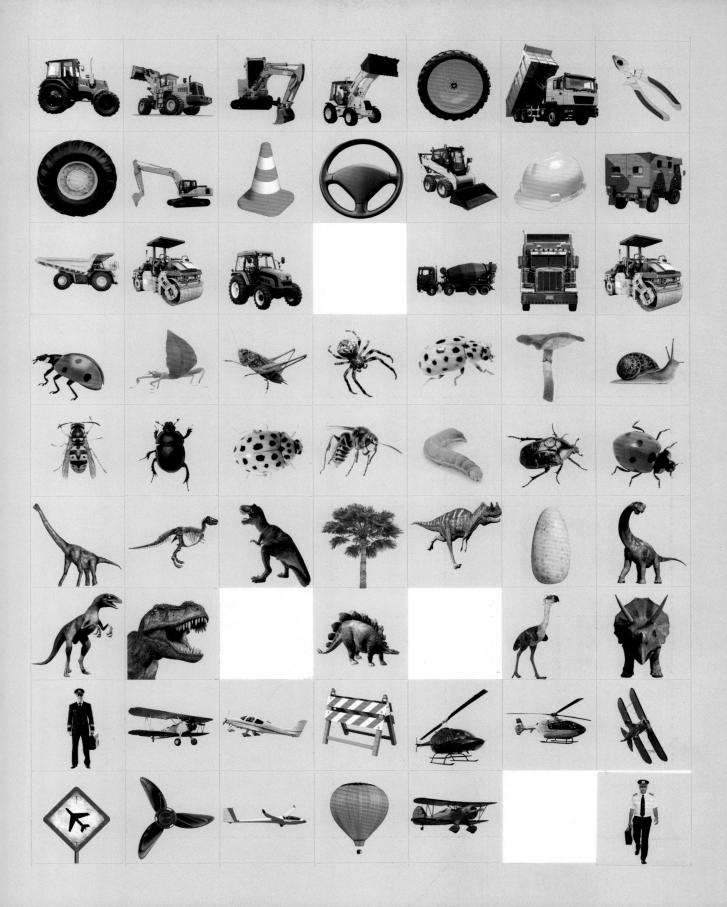

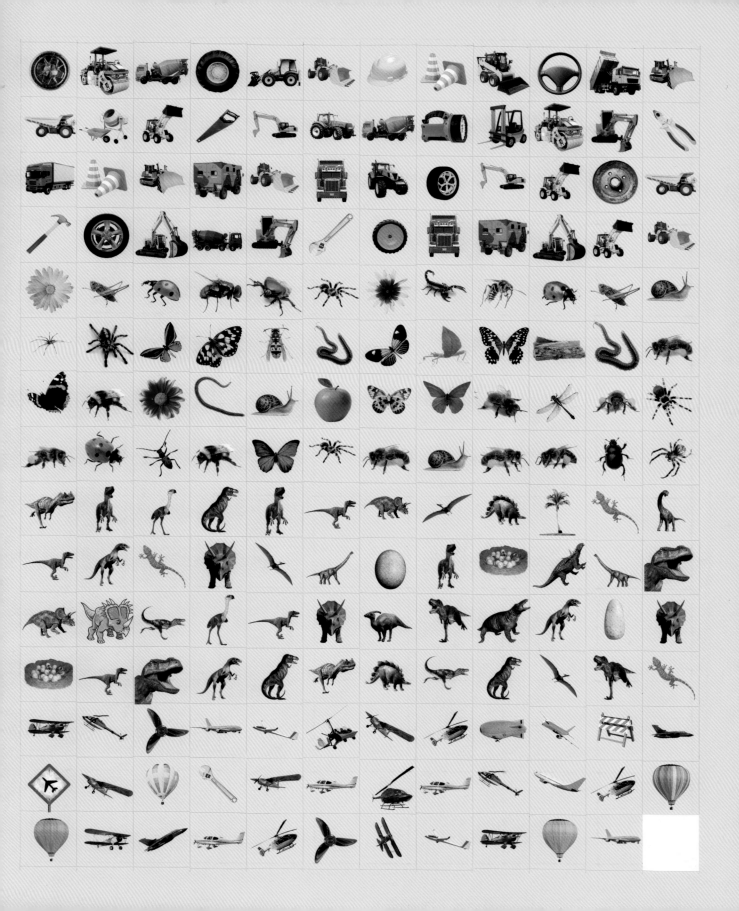

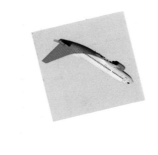

Dino Doodles

Use these scaly shapes to create your own awesome dinosaurs! See the example below.

JOKE CORNER

Q. How can you tell there's a Stegosaurus in your refrigerator?

A: The door won't close!

Prehistoric Fun

Try playing this memory game with your friends and family.

The first player says something like...

The next player repeats the phrase and adds something else...

'My dinosaur has a really long neck.'

'My dinosaur has a really long neck and sharp claws.'

The game continues with each person repeating the whole phrase and adding something new...

'My dinosaur has a really long neck, sharp claws and a large tail'.

If someone forgets something, or says it wrong, they're out. The last person still playing is the winner.

Dino Dots

Join the dots and discover a cool dinosaur!

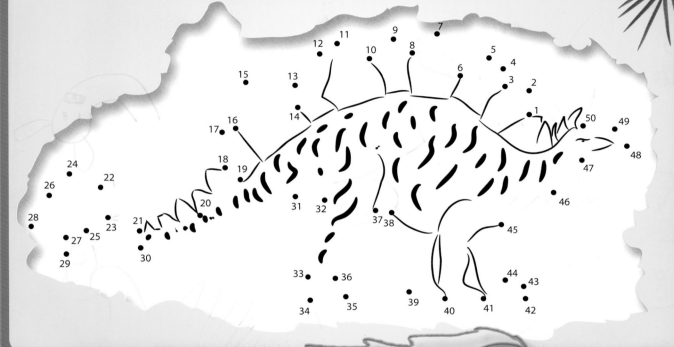

Shadow Match

Can you spot which of these shadows matches the dinosaur?

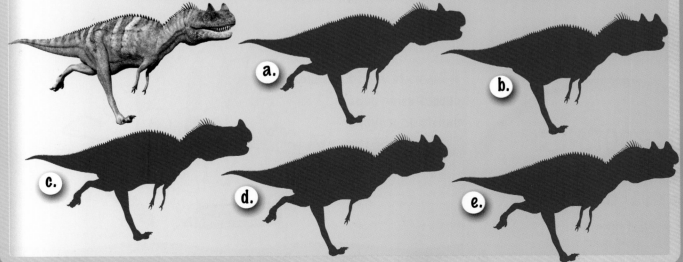

a.

b.

c.

d.

e.

Dinosaur Puppet

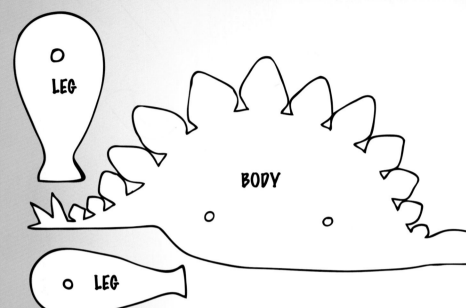

LEG

BODY

LEG

You will need:

Tracing paper

Pencil

Thin card

Scissors

Paper fasteners

Pens or paint or crayons

1 Trace over the legs and body and transfer them onto pieces of cardboard. Ask an adult to cut out the shapes from the cardboard.

2 Ask an adult to pierce holes in the cardboard in the places shown on the templates. Push paper fasteners through the holes to fix the dinosaur together.

3 Decorate your dinosaur puppet using pens or paints or crayons.

JOKE CORNER

Q. What dinosaur could jump higher than a house?

A. All of them. Houses can't jump!

52

Dinosaur Race

Can you work out which of these dinosaurs will get to the tasty lizard first?
Count the number of footprints, the one with the fewest footprints is the quickest.

a.

b.

c.

JOKE CORNER

Q. What do you call
a Tyrannosaurus
that talks and talks
and talks?

A. A dino-bore!

Draw a Diplodocus

Follow these easy steps to draw a Diplodocus.

Draw a diplodocus in the space below.

Whose Tail?

Can you work out which tail belongs to which dinosaur?

Raptor Race

Instructions

Players: 2–4
You will need:
Coins to use as counters and a die.

Each player should choose a dino sticker from the sticker sheets and stick it to their counter.
Place the counters on the start space.
Take it in turns to roll the die and move your counter forward that many spaces.
The first player to land on the finish square is the winner!

Start

1

2
Stop to munch some leaves. Miss a turn.

3

4

5

6
Chase a dinosaur. Move forward 2 steps.

7

8

9

1

Terror Tracks

Can you draw lines to match up each pair of footprints?

Mega Maze

Help the dinosaur find the nest by drawing a path through the maze?

Jigsaw Jumble

Can you spot which pieces complete this dinosaur jigsaw?

a.

b.

c.

d.

e.

Odd One Out

Can you spot which of these dinosaurs is the odd one out?
What is different about it?

a.

b.

c.

d.

Spot the Difference

Can you spot the **5** differences between these two dino pictures?

a

b

Decorating Dinosaurs

Here are 5 cool dinosaur outlines.
Use pens to decorate each dinosaur.

Half and Half

Can you match these halves of dinosaurs together?

a.

b.

c.

d.

e.

f.

g.

h.

Dinosaur Dinner Time

Follow the trails to discover what each dinosaur is having for its dinner.

1. Velociraptor

2. Brachiosaurus

3. Stegosaurus

4. T. rex

a.

b.

c.

d.

JOKE CORNER

Q. When can three dinosaurs fit under an umbrella and not get wet?

A. When it's not raining!

Mystery Dinosaur

Can you work out which dinosaur is a Stegosaurus by following the clues?

Clue 1
I do not fly.

Clue 2
I walk on four legs.

Clue 3
I have not got a long neck.

Clue 4
I have spines on my back.

a.

b.

c.

d.

e.

Amazing Flyers

Count how many red, blue and yellow aircraft are in the sky.
Write your answers in the white circles.

red

7

blue

3

yellow

4

Perfect Paper Glider

You will need: a sheet of A4 paper

Follow these easy instructions to create a paper glider plane.

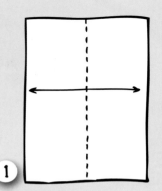

1

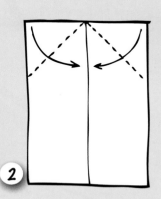

2

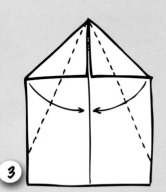

3

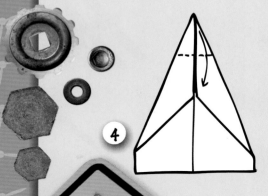

4

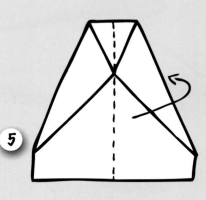

5

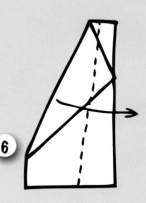

6

Front and Back

Can you match up the front of the aircraft with their backs?

a.

b.

d.

c.

1.

2.

3.

4.

Odd One Out

Can you work out which of these pictures of helicopters is the odd one out?
What is different about it?

a.

b.

c.

d.

e.

f.

Plane Patterns

Can you draw the next plane in the sequence?

1.

2.

3.

4.

Aircraft Close-Ups

Can you spot which close-up is of which aircraft?

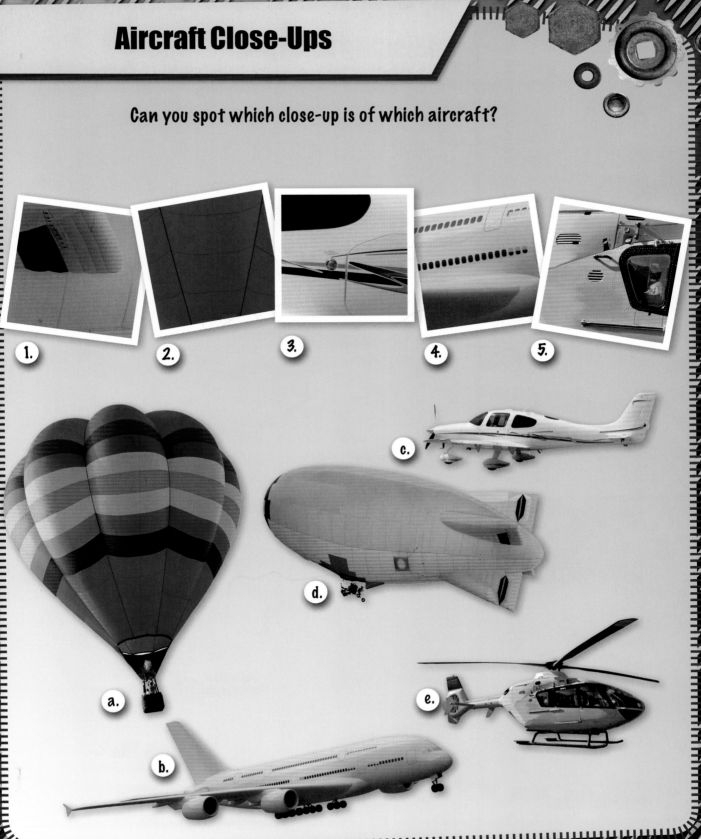

1.

2.

3.

4.

5.

a.

b.

c.

d.

e.

Missing Aircraft

Can you spot which aircraft is missing from box b? Which is the new aircraft that has appeared in box b?

Fantastic Fighter Jet

Follow these easy steps to draw a fighter jet.

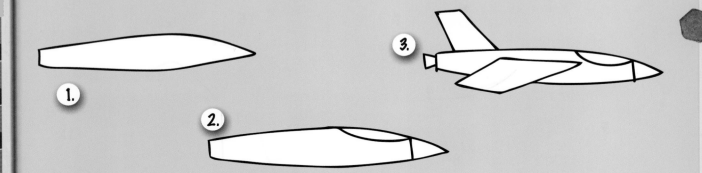

Try drawing some fighter jets in the space below.

Cloud Hopping

Can you help this hot-air balloon down to the ground by only moving through the clouds with even numbers?

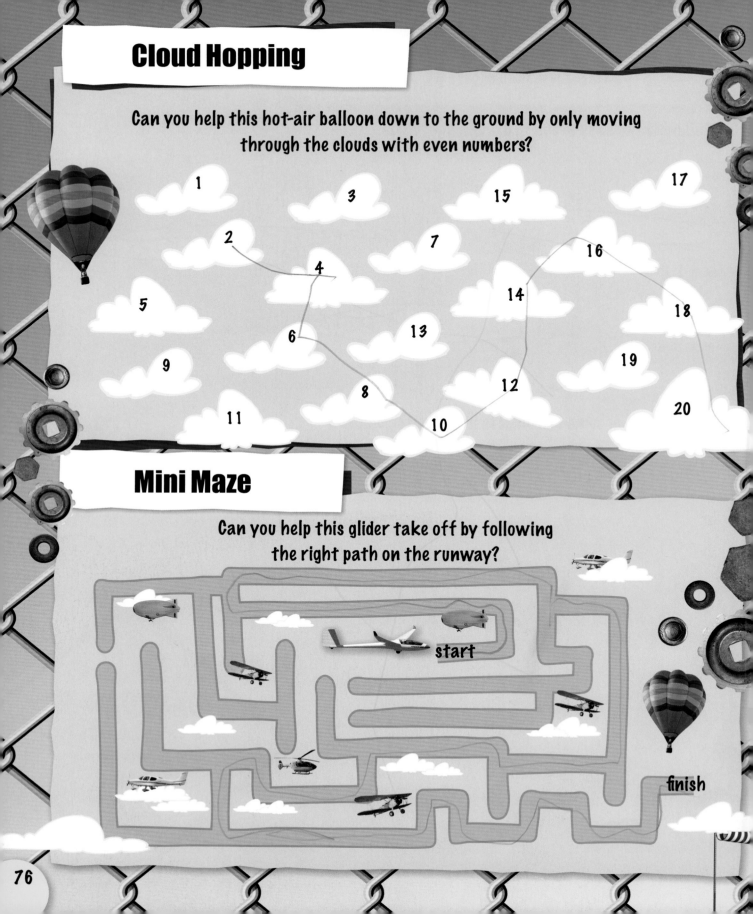

1 3 15 17
2 7 16
4 14
5 18
6 13
9 8 12 19
11 10 20

Mini Maze

Can you help this glider take off by following the right path on the runway?

start

finish

Follow the Trails

Follow the trails to see which pilot is flying which aircraft.

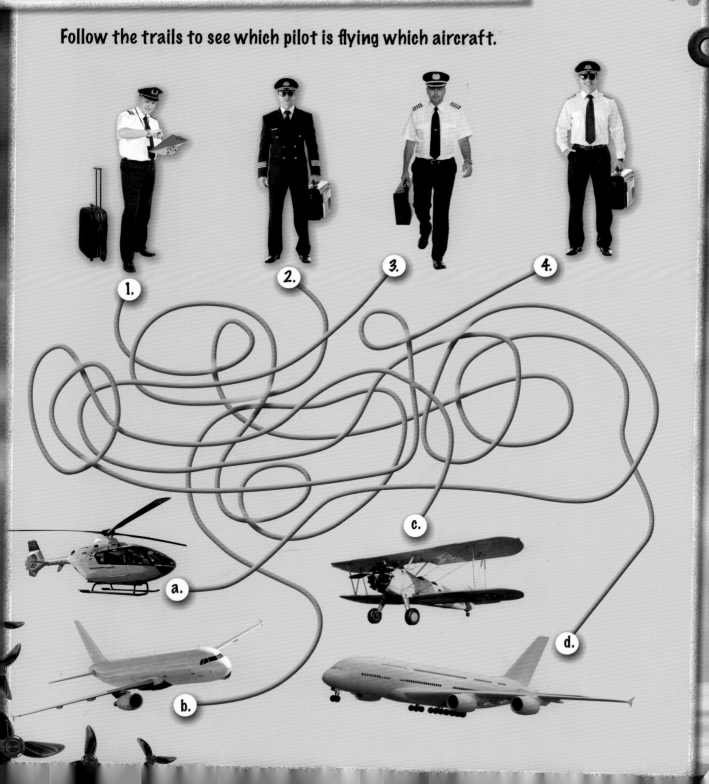

Match the Pair

Can you match the pairs of gliders?

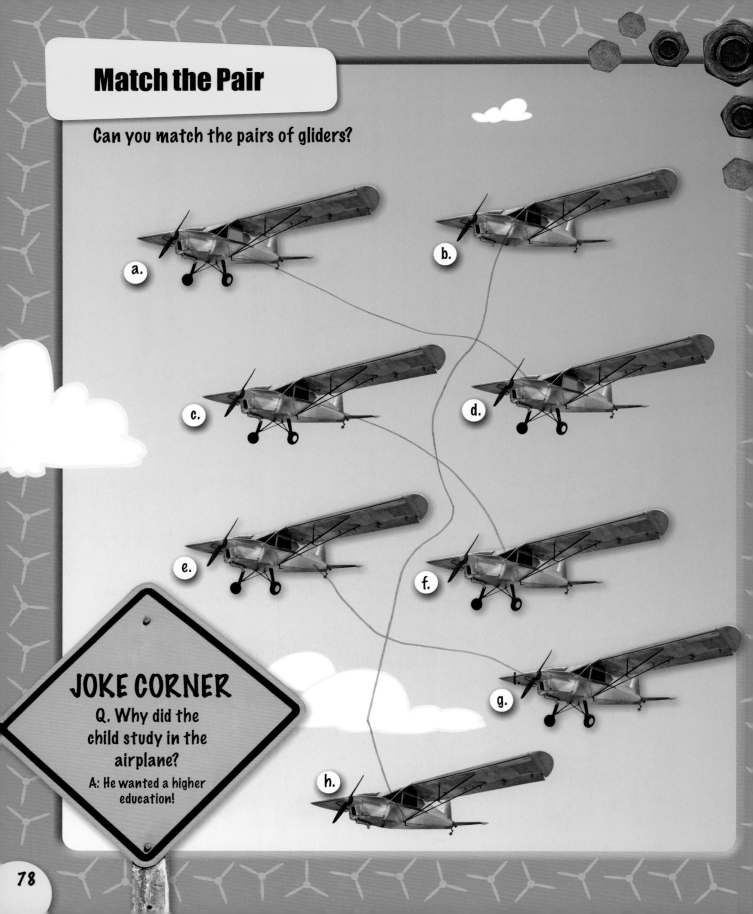

a.

b.

c.

d.

e.

f.

g.

h.

JOKE CORNER
Q. Why did the child study in the airplane?
A: He wanted a higher education!

Make a Hot-Air Balloon

1

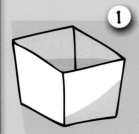

Ask an adult to cut the top from a small cardboard box. This will become the balloon's basket.

2

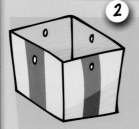

Ask an adult to punch a hole in each of the basket's sides. You can now decorate the basket with paints or by covering it in craft paper.

You will need:

A balloon
A cardboard box
Wool
Scissors
Craft paper
Glue
Scissors
Paints

3

Now cut 4 pieces of wool to the same size (30cm/ 12 inches). Tie each piece of wool to a hole in the basket.

4

Now blow up the balloon and knot the end. You can now tie the wool onto the end of the balloon!

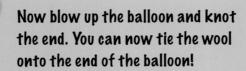

Flying Home

The airplanes are racing back to the airport, but who will make it back first and win?

Instructions

Two friends can play this game. Each must choose a sticker and place it onto a coin. This will become the counter. You will also need a dice.

1. Put both aircraft at the start.
2. Take turns to roll the dice and move your counter forward.
3. If you land on the lightning miss a go.
4. If you land on the sun or a white cloud go forward one space.
5. The first aircraft to get to the finish wins!

6

5

4

3

2

1

Start

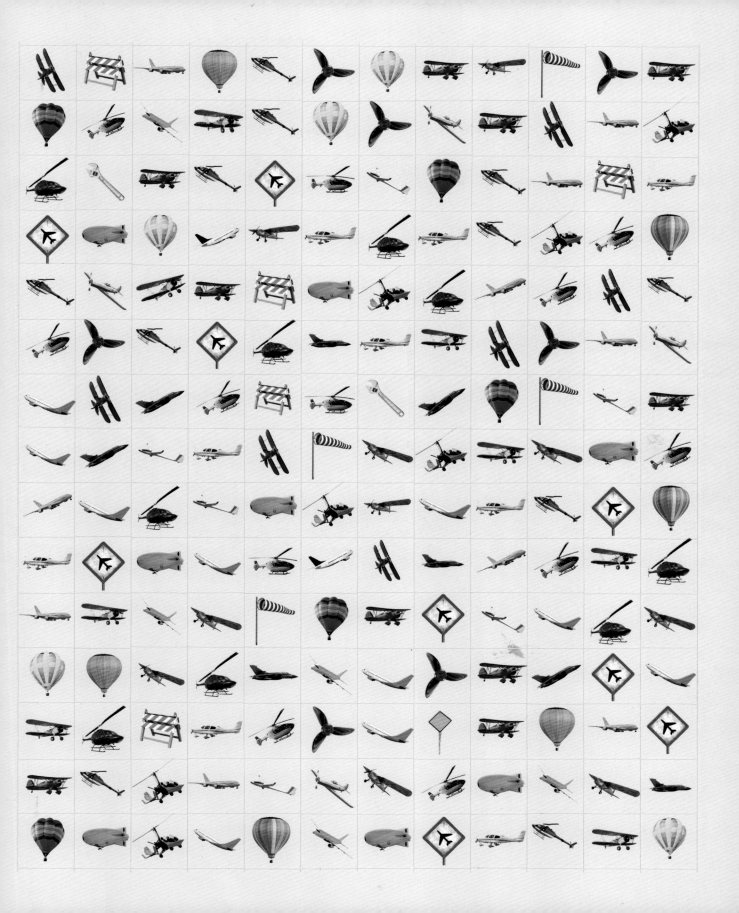

Memory Game

Study this picture for 30 seconds, then cover it and try to answer the questions at the bottom of the page.

1. How many hot-air balloons were there?
2. Did the passenger jet have a red or blue tail?
3. How many passengers were in the microlight?
4. Which aircraft was yellow?
5. How many aircraft in total where on the page?

Dot-to-Dot

Join the dots and then decorate this fighter jet.

JOKE CORNER

Q. What type of air do the richest airplanes fly in?

A. Million-air!

Design Your Own Plane

Draw a picture of a really cool plane, then use your best pens to decorate it!

Plane Crazy

Copy this plane into the grid square by square?
When you've finished, why not decorate it with your pens?

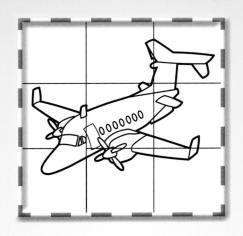

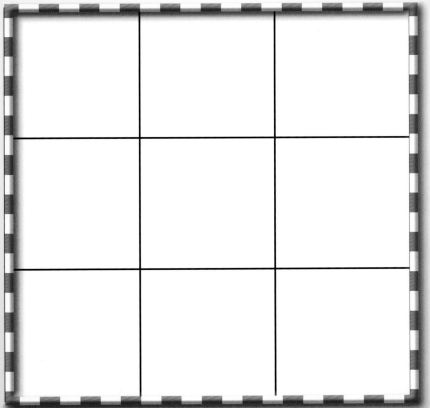

Picture Puzzle

Can you work out which picture should go in each square of the puzzle?
Each picture should only appear once in each row and column.

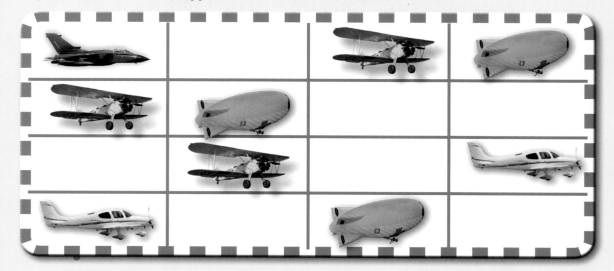

Can you work out which plane will take off first?
The lines with the fewest flags will be quickest.

Who Wins?

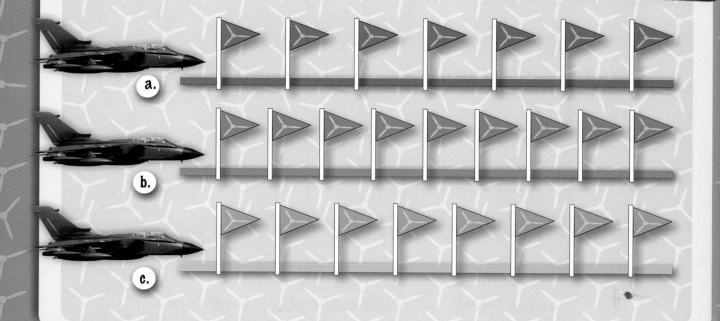

Maze Madness

Can you find your way through this maze
of clouds to the airport at the other end?

start

finish

Shadow Match

Can you match the shadows to the aircraft?

1.

2.

3.

a.

c.

c.

True or False?

Can you work out which of these questions are true and which are false? Write T or F in the white boxes.

1. A hot air balloon has two wings. F

2. A sea plane can land on water. T

3. A hang glider has an engine. F

4. An airplane has three sets of wheels. F

JOKE CORNER

Q. What did the man say when he walked into the airplane?

A. Ouch!

The Bigger Picture

Can you match each close-up image to the correct aircraft below?

1.

2.

3.

4.

5.

a.

b.

c.

d.

e.

Paper Plate Mobile

1. Follow the instructions on page 80 and draw five hot-air balloons on craft paper. Ask an adult to cut out your drawings.

2. Fold a paper plate in half. Ask an adult to pierce 5 holes along the fold. Thread different lengths of wool through these holes. You can now tape the plate closed.

3. Ask an adult to pierce holes in the top of each of your hot-air balloons and then thread and knot the wool through the holes.

4. Now you can hang your mobile up and see the hot-air balloons floating in the sky.

Plane Designer

Use your best pens to decorate this picture.

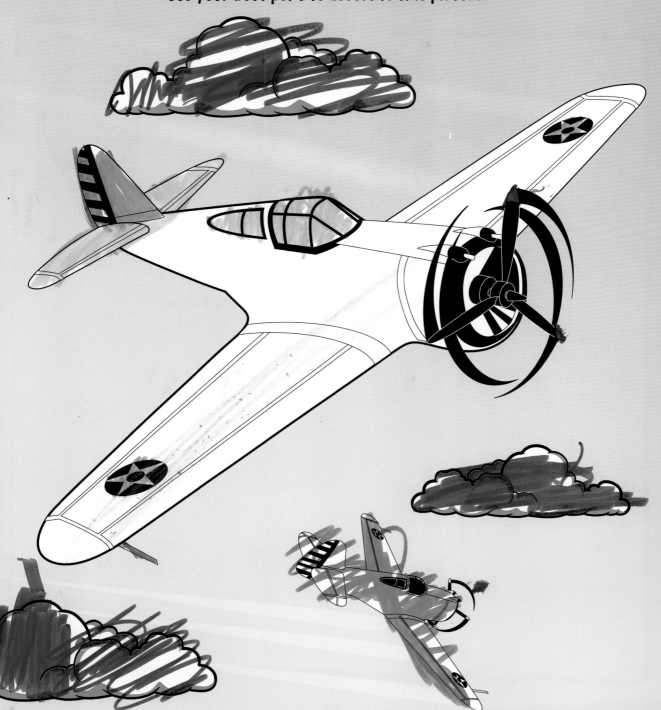

Drawing Hot-Air Balloons!

Follow these easy steps to draw perfect hot-air balloons!

1.
2.
3.
4.
5.

Try drawing hot-air balloons in the space below:

Answers

Answers

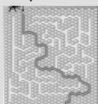

Answers

Page **54** Dino Duos: A and E, B and I, C and N, D and L, F and Q, G and O, H and R, J and M, K and P,
S doesn't have a pair.

Page **55** Mega Maze:

Page **56** Terror Tracks: A and M, B and V, C and W, D and Q, E and L, F and K, G and P, H and X, I and T, J and S, N and U, O and R

Page **57** Dinosaur Race: A

Page **59** Whose Tail?: 1 and D, 2 and C, 3 and A, 4 and B

Page **62** Crazy Close-Ups: 1 and C, 2 and B, 3 and A, 4 and D

Page **63** Jigsaw Jumble: Odd One Out: D, it is missing the plates on its tail.

Page **64** Spot the Difference:

Page **66** Half and Half: A and F, B and G, C and H, D and E

Page **67** Dinosaur Dinner Time: 1 and A, 2 and B, 3 and D, 4 and C

Page **68** Mystery Dinosaur: C

Page **69** Amazing Flyers: 7 red , 3 blue, 4 yellow

Page **71** Front and Back: A and 4, B and 2, C and 1, D and 3   Odd One Out: D, it is missing its propeller.

Answers

Page **72** Plane Patterns: 1.  , 2. , 3. , 4.

Page **73** Aircraft Close-Ups: 1 and D, 2 and A, 3 and C, 4 and B, 5 and E

Page **74** Missing Aircraft:

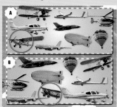

Page **76** Cloud Hopping:

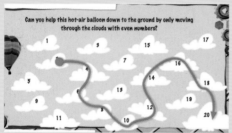

Mini Maze:

Page **77** Follow the Trails: 1 and D, 2 and B, 3 and A, 4 and C

Page **78** Match the Pair: A and D, B and H, C and F, E and G

Page **82** Memory Game: 1. 4, 2. Red, 3. Helicopter, 4. 7 aircraft

Page **86** Picture puzzle:

Who Wins?: A

Page **87** Maze Madness:

Page **88** Shadow Match: 1 and C, 2 and A, 3 and C   True or False?: 1. False, 2. True, 3. False, 4. True

Page **89** The Bigger Picture: 1 and B, 2 and D, 3 and C, 4 and E, 5 and A